WITNESS

2017–2020

Selections

Hilton Obenzinger

Irene Weinberger Books

Library of Congress Cataloging-in-Publication Data

Names: Obenzinger, Hilton, author.
Title: Witness : California, 2017-2020 : selections / Hilton Obenzinger.
Description: Maplewood, NJ : Irene Weinberger Books, 2021. | Summary:
"Selection of poems 2017-2020 before and during the pandemic and the
California wildfires"-- Provided by publisher.
Identifiers: LCCN 2021005555 | ISBN 9780990376798 (trade paperback)
Subjects: LCGFT: Poetry.
Classification: LCC PS3565.B36 W58 2021 | DDC 811/.54--dc23
LC record available at https://lccn.loc.gov/2021005555

Many of these poems were posted on Facebook and appeared in *Best American Poetry, Café Review, Heron Clan, Meredith Sue Willis's Books for Readers, Musings of a Pandemic, Tikkun*, and other journals.

Cover photograph: Alan Senauke. San Francisco Bay, Berkeley, September 9, 2020

Interior Design WSM Books

Copyediting: Elissa Rabellino

Irene Weinberger Books
An imprint of Hamilton Stone Editions
P.O. Box 43, Maplewood, NJ 07040
www.ireneweinbergerbooks.com/

Also by Hilton Obenzinger

A Cinch: Amazing Works from the Columbia Review, edited with Les Gottesman and Alan Senauke

Thunder Road

Bright Lights! Big City!

Beyond Up and Down, with Les Gottesman and Alan Senauke

The Day of the Exquisite Poet Is Kaput

This Passover or the Next I Will Never Be in Jerusalem

New York on Fire

Cannibal Eliot and the Lost Histories of San Francisco

a*hole: a novel

Running through Fire: How I Survived the Holocaust [oral history by Zosia Goldberg]

American Palestine: Melville, Twain, and the Holy Land Mania

Busy Dying

Beginning: The Immigration Poems, 1924–1926, of Nachman Obzinger [editor]

How We Write: The Varieties of Writing Experience

Treyf Pesach [Unkosher Passover]

Remembering

Diane di Prima
Les Gottesman
Corky Lee

TABLE OF CONTENTS

**PART TWO
CORONA CHRONICLES
2020**

PART THREE
TESTIMONY
November 2020–January 2021

WITNESS

2017–2020

Selections

Preface

The Grand Canyon of San Francisco

November 2015–January 2016

I had a dream that I was walking through beautiful woods with Moses. Not Charlton Heston but more like the old graybeard Walt Whitman. We walked and talked and then came upon a flat expanse of shimmering gold like a body of water. It was bright and beautiful, and then I put my foot on it to test if it was shallow or deep. The gold turned to black, and Moses gasped, "You just killed God!" At that point I woke up.

Has anyone ever had a dream that they've killed God? I've never had such a dream, so I'm checking to see if it's common or not. I don't know what to make of it. What would Emanuel Swedenborg think?

Another dream: Visited print shop (I used to be a printing press operator), a busy place, then I was taken out for a walk in SF with a friend (no one recognizable) and in Glen Park we came upon a valley with high red rock walls like stalagmites and stalactites, stunning, with playgrounds on the bottom. I was astounded. "What neighborhood is this? I've never seen this in San Francisco," and my friend responded that this was the Grand Canyon of San Francisco . . . The dream went on to visit a decorative flan shop (flan in the shape of birds, things like that). I asked how much and the owner (Anglo) avoided telling me. Then I walked on with my friend, who I realized was a transgender woman with muscular arms and chest. OK, that's a mild surprise compared to the Grand Canyon.

By this time I was exhausted and had to wake up. It's getting to be too tiring to sleep, and I need to stay awake to avoid falling into the Grand Canyon of San Francisco.

Here's a dream while visiting Stella's sister Muriel in Carmel Valley: I walk from one room through a doorway to another but then forget why I went into the room. I realize that this is common for people as they age. But then I also realize that I just died. I left the room through the doorway but don't know why I came. End of dream. When I woke up,¹ I realized I dreamt of my own death. But I also understood that the experience in the dream could apply to being born. Remind me: why did we enter this room?

One last dream: Walking around Lower Manhattan where my father's textile business was located, Broadway south of Canal a couple of blocks. I was making geologic risk assessments, like earthquakes, with my brother (NYC has actually had earthquakes). Meanwhile we tried to get something to eat but the meal was just a block, freeze-dried, and we dragged this frozen block around on a string until we got to a restaurant where the chef softened it up and cooked it into a stew. We were happy and ready to pay for it when Donald Trump walked in and offered to pay the chef, handing over a ten or twenty dollar bill. The chef wanted him to autograph the bill but Trump said it was public property and offered to autograph his apron.

At this point I wake up—puzzled and pissed off. Trump has entered my dreams! *Goddamn it, Trump, stay out of my dreams!* It's enough that your head fills up TV screens. I hereby resign from dreams.

PART ONE

FACIAL RECOGNITION

2017–2019

Houston, We Have a Problem

Hurricane Harvey

September 2, 2017

Houston, we have a problem
Houston, are you there? Houston, do *you* have a problem?
If you have a problem, what the hell are *we* supposed to do?
Houston, you're the one to guide us, and now you have sunk
Earth to Houston, are you there?
Come in, please
Earth to Houston—please stay alive
Houston, it's 106 degrees in San Francisco, unheard of
Never been that hot, ever
Houston, the fires surround us, the smoke closes in
And you are swept away in a storm
Houston, you are sprawled across the Gulf
Like a patient etherized on a table
We laugh for you, but we know the ordeal continues
We laugh with floods and fires and earthquakes,
With gases and flows
Maybe Houston knows
Houston, will you guide us to another planet?
Houston, we have a problem

Let's Shoot

November 6, 2017

Let's go to church and shoot
Let's go to the movies and shoot
Let's go to the music festival
Let's go to the supermarket
Let's go to the school
Let's go to the aquarium and shoot out the glass
And have people drown while we shoot them
And don't forget to shoot the fish
Let's go to the museum and shoot Art
And then shoot the people looking at Picasso
Let's shoot Picasso
He's dead so let's go to the cemetery and shoot the dead
Let's go to the Halls of Justice and shoot all the judges
Let's go to the NRA HQ and shoot everyone
Let's go to the moon and shoot Earth
Let's get drunk and shoot
Let's pray and shoot
Let's go to the hospital and shoot the sick
Let's get naked and shoot
Let's shoot naked people
Let's get an AR-15 and shoot people we hate
Let's shoot people we love
Let's never run out of bullets
Let's never run out of long guns automatics machine guns
Let's get a truckload of grenade launchers
If only we had tanks and missiles
Let's shoot while the shooting lasts
So much to shoot and so little time
Let's shoot the small quiet wind
That blows through our hearts
And kill it good

The Count

November 16, 2017

Men! It's time to take a count:
There's a president
There's another president
There's the current president
Who says "Believe me" and grabs
Then there's the senator
There's the Hollywood mogul
(Do we know what a mogul is?)
Then there's the comic, the doctor
There's another comic
There's the senator who used to be a comic
Then there's the actor
And there's a director
Of course there's the priest and the teacher
There's a professor also
And another professor
And another
There's an even older president
There's the Sunday School teacher
There's a pastor minister rabbi guru
Here comes another president
The famous writer, all the celebrity
Crackpots are here too
There's the student
There's the guy at the copy machine
There's the guy who cleans the office
Then another senator
A candidate for Congress
There's a very rich man
There's a not so rich man
Chalk up another senator
We could be here all night
Every man needs to dig deep
That means me too
There are pinches
There's "seduction"

There's the grab
There's the glad hand
There's all of this and more
Each man and more
Now–no more
Stop
One more president and that's it
Done and over and out
Keep your hands to yourself
Stop
Welcome to a new social contract
Sign on the zipper

Warning

False alarm in Hawaii

January 13, 2018

Warning! A missile is coming your way
Stand outside with arms up to catch
The radiation and cure your headache
Oh say can you see
All the way up the sky's inferno
Warning a war is happening right now
And has been happening for decades
No need for a missile, plenty dead already
False alarm
Return to your daily blinding flash

Old Men with Canes

June 12, 2018

I've joined the club of old men with canes
I hadn't realized it until Mr. Pain struck me down
Tossed me in with the wrecks at the junkyard
I never noticed before all the limping hobbling old guys
There are women on crutches and walkers too
Gray-haired travelers sitting on scooters
But it's old men with canes that are my tribe
We wink at each other as we pass
We know what it's like
How all of life has slowed down by necessity
But allowing for an amusing illusion of choice
We shuffle off to Buffalo or Palo Alto
With a cane and the past
None of the kids would believe
What we once did
How we outran the cops
Stood long hours operating machines
Shot at shadows in the jungle
Now obstacles loom like icebergs
Steps and doors and sex and crosswalks
Standing at a urinal trying to engineer
My fly while holding a cane
Now some old guys with crooked legs and hips
Tilt with their canes
Limp like old sports
Some need to keep balance with a stick
A little vertigo after decades of dizzy gravity
Yanking our spines down to our ankles
Others constantly curse Mr. Pain
Bent low over their canes
Horizontal emblems of time gone
Mr. Pain visits me just like he does the others
Mr. Pain is not mean just does his job
Clutches legs and crushes backs
A companion always loyal
But Mr. Pain's no fool he's the glue

That holds all the canes together
He's the sergeant at arms for this club
Welcome to my back, Mr. Pain
Can I invite you for a walk?
And beat your head in with my stick?

All Regrets

As surgery approaches

August 26, 2018

I'm no Edith Piaf
I regret everything
And I will miss so much
Life on earth has its wonders
Flowers and doughnuts
Blessings of early morning air
Before all the wildfires
Greet us with waves of smoke
I will count my failures
And give away my blessings too
And laugh
Thank you all
I never did accomplish anything
Some love
And a little kindness
And that's pretty good

Revolutionary Letter

For Diane di Prima

October 5, 2018

You're a Christian in Nazi Germany
And Jesus demands
You disobey the orders for hatred and war
Even as those around you laugh at murder

You're a Jew during the Warsaw Ghetto Uprising
You know you will die but at least
A lesson will be delivered to the monsters

You're a Palestinian still holding on to the key to your home
Hold it for decades, ready to return, keeping steadfast
How many years will the people of Gaza be caged?

How many years will the children at the border be caged?
How long will they be stolen from their parents?

It's 1939 Spain and you're in the antifascist underground
Can you even think of life without the Generalissimo?
Any day Franco will die, even if it takes decades

You're a slave in 1825 in North Carolina
Freedom is a dream but dreams can't be enslaved
And you flee to the Great Dismal Swamp
Where the slave masters fear to go

Your people have been driven from your homeland
Shedding tears along the trail for hundreds of miles
Yet your people still hold together,
Ready to build beyond tears, beyond massacres
Even though Andrew Jackson wants you to disappear
But you refuse

You're a woman raped by a rich college boy
Powerful men won't believe you but millions do
You are not alone, you will learn how many women and men
Roar with disbelief and rage and begin to act

No one should despair—and everyone should despair
No one should fall in tears—and everyone should sob
No one should lose hope—even though hope eludes us
No one should mourn—even as we mourn our losses

Others have suffered, others have endured
Many have been murdered, many jailed, many ignored
Many have lived all their lives under the rule of hatred

We can't pay the price of freedom with credit cards
We pay for freedom with our souls, with our bodies
Get ready to overcome the horror
Get ready to fight like hell
In open and hidden ways

Do not accept the orders for hatred and war
Get ready to survive
Outlast the reign of rapists, con men, and murderers
Surviving is the first road to freedom
Surviving is the revenge of the just
You too will survive

They Dragged the Autistic Kid across the Floor

October 15, 2018

They dragged the autistic kid across the floor
They interrogated the journalist
Accidentally they murdered him
A black man tries to go into his apartment building
A white woman calls the police
Why is this dark frightening man making believe
He lives in my beautiful building?
The president declares that he's not a baby
Babies in Yemen die right before our eyes
Gaza is still a prison
More protesters are shot by snipers
But the Realtor Prince will convince the Desert Prince
That they can buy peace
As soon as Yemen is destroyed
What wonderful beachfront property in Gaza
What glittering resorts could be built there
There is definitely hope
Even if the planet is accidentally murdered

Old People Endlessly Talk About Their Health

October 25, 2018

My liver bounces around like a basketball
My kidneys circle my head like moons
I can't find my penis, buried somewhere in those flaps
I can't find my vagina, dark and deep
With a middle school soccer team
Waiting patiently inside
My intestines are playing cat's cradle
My prostate is knitting a shroud
For my bladder
Or maybe it's the other way around
My heart has been spitting on the sidewalk
Love stabbed it and the doctors did the rest
Nobody loves lungs better than toes
As my respiratory system dangles off the side of my feet
Waiting for the sharks to bite
I have a gallbladder that likes to play marbles
(You *still* have a gall bladder?)
And then there's Breast Cancer
Slicing across the land
CANCER—CANCER—CANCER
So many different types of cancer that
Jesus fed the tumors to the guests at a wedding
They thought it was loaves and fishes
Testicular cancer: What would Jesus do about that?
Pancreatic cancer has a datebook that marks
How long I have to live
But I can't find out because my eyes
Are spread across the highway like roadkill
My uterus went out on an errand and never came back
I have varicose veins that can be plucked
To play the "Flight of the Bumblebee"
I have a bald skull that leaks wrong aphorisms
Don't forget the knees and the hips
As they walk off into the sunset
I need a strict accounting of
All that's gone

Facial Recognition

April 28, 2019

I'm looking for facial recognition
Does anyone recognize my face?
Do I have a face?
I want to wander through the streets like Baudelaire
And recognize my face everywhere
But I look around and I can't tell if
I'm seeing the face of America
I see the face of slave catchers and metaphysical Indian killers
The face of whips and fists and gun butts
The face of an angry white boy shooting up synagogues
The face of liars and haters
Walt Whitman can embrace all the liars and haters
Because he got multitudes to spare
But I don't want my lone face with them
I'm not broadminded like Whitman
I'd like to see the Face of God like Emily Dickinson
But I don't want to die in a storm of bullets
I'd like to sport a smart glad Frank O'Hara martini face
Without getting run over by a beach buggy
I want the face of the Rebel Girl and Mother Jones
The face of Martin and Malcolm
All the faces on the Women's March 2017
Those should be enough faces
To recognize the great danger that I pose

After Capitalism Is Gone

July 5, 2019

1

All the children will come home
All the mothers and fathers will come home
All the gangs will put their guns away
All the politicians will forget how to lie
All the soldiers will forget how to shoot
All work will become joy
All joy will become love
All the poems and plays
Will wipe the tears from our eyes
Shakespeare will finally be paid all he's worth
All the housekeepers will get paid all they're worth
All species will loaf and laugh
Animals Birds Fish
All will take it easy
All our breaths will rise and fall
All the dead will return to their tombs, satisfied
All the rivers will be pure and alive
All the rulers and the rich will be forgotten
We will be able to go to the supermarket
And buy groceries
With our good looks

2

Welcome to the Great Museum of Capital
Here are the archives
All the ephemera and inflated ideas
All the cruel rationales
Here are hunks of labor congealed into money
Paychecks and pink slips are attached to the walls
Relics of a time when we had to rely
On the good graces of investors and bosses
Bankers are pinned to display cases like butterflies
Police cars and armored cars are nailed to the floor
Fossil fuels have become fossils once again

In the Museum you can ponder
Displays of plastic water bottles
Heaped into giant piles
And pet rocks
You can contemplate the portraits
Of those who stole freedom
Paintings of those who stole our bodies
In slave ships and tenements
Fools who stole from all future generations
Without a thought or a care
In the portrait gallery they look like ordinary people
Sitting in their chairs with small dogs
On their laps
When we enter the Museum of Capital we are shocked
But when we leave we are grateful
To be alive in a world where all of this is gone
Readiness is all
That's true
And we had been ready for centuries
And ripeness is all, too
We drop from trees like heavy fruit
And have no idea how we became so sweet
Once we threw off Profit

3

Now that capitalism is gone
We can cross the border of exchange value
And discover that there are no borders
And no exchange
And all of our work is valued
It's hard to tell where one's genitals end
And your neighbor's tender places begin
At least according to Karl Marx's 1844 manuscripts
The division of labor in the sexual act
No longer divides
Once there was a bookstore named "Borders"
And that made no difference at all
Once you cross into a book there are no maps
You need to find your way out through your wits
And your vocabulary

People throughout the world forget
The lines that used to cut across our bodies
And today we walk across every border
Into each other's arms

The Great Replacement Theory

August 5, 2019

How much grief can people take? Are we there yet? Is this the shape of civil war, at least one aspect? Whenever we walk down a street and see a young white man should we cross to the other side? Lock your car doors when passing a group of young white men? If we see a young white man with a backpack, should we call the police because it could be a firearm? White men have been the purveyors of violence for centuries—as slave catchers, Indian killers, lynch mobs, etc.—and now young white men have taken up the mantle. The fact is, young white men believe they are the targets of the "replacement" paranoid fantasy, since they believe they are the ones being replaced, and more of them are increasingly unhinged.

I first was baffled by the notion of replacement when I heard in Virginia the Nazis chant "Jews will not replace us." Huh? What do Jews have to do with a statue of Robert E. Lee? But then I came to understand the whole paranoid fantasy: liberal Jews are promoting multiculturalism, immigration, and the like, with the aim of replacing white people. Ridiculous. But then I thought about it, and it wouldn't be such a bad idea to replace Nazis with solid hard-working Mexicans. So, there is a place for replacement. And there's a place in Hell for mass murderers.

Inscribe the Planet

Rosh Hashanah

September 19, 2019

The fullness of the Earth has been gouged
Clear-cut, strip-mined, pumped dry
The rains have stolen the sun
And spread before us harsh burning plastic
Birds migrate to a different universe
Gone from our trees
And we can't learn their songs
And of those trees the giant redwood trees are torn
Their red flesh unraveling before our eyes
There is no sweet honey in which to dip our apples
The bees choke on toxic grief
And the trees don't bear fruit
What have we done without thinking?
When thinking is supposed to be
The blessing of our kind
Why did we invent science if we don't use it?
How can we heal the world?
How can we quiet the awful storms?

The moon and the sun wheel around again
It's a new year of revolutions
Cheer the celestial bodies on
And welcome our terrestrial body
We can try to heal the fractured glaciers
Keep whole the many species still alive
We can free us of our own undoing
We can stand on the threshold
Between what we knew and what we hope to know
Between darkness and light
Between foolish and wise
We can stand in the doorway
Between hope and despair
And take a deep breath
And pray that Creation will sustain the planet
And all that live upon it

How will we mourn the cities that will drown?
Gone under the waters of Babylon
Under Congo Mississippi Nile
Can we weep for the islands sinking to the ocean floor?
How will we remember all that is gone?
How will we dream of all that has been lost?
Is there an index to the Book of Life?
Look up all references to carrier pigeons and ancient tribes
How can we restore the pulse of the planet?
Is there CPR for the Four Directions?

Only by holding each other in dismay and delight
Only by knowing the truth can we heal
All the poisoned rivers and all the weeping ice caps
Only by loving ourselves as part of all
Only by acting as a species conscious of itself
Only by doing all that needs to be done
Can we inscribe the Earth in the Book of Life

The Planet on September 26, 2084

September 26, 2019

1

Las Vegas is nonstop hot blowtorch
And all bets are off
Phoenix is nowhere
The bird has yet to rise from the ashes
Every day the bird lunges up but collapses in a heap
Miami is great through the glass-bottom boat
The Pacific is an open patch
In a dense floating continent of melting plastic
New Orleans is a covered stadium
In the mouth of the continent
Mardi Gras is celebrated in submarines
Mars is populated with refugees
Earth is so bad that Mars is a relief
Oklahoma has gone underground
Because of constant tornadoes
Although the subterranean dwellers
Are met with earthquakes
Triggered by incessant fracking
Trees have lost their way
And there are no birds to show them where to go
Fish gag on tiny plastic dust
Rivers run dry or have become massive lakes
Swimmers glide between the high Sierra Nevada islands
No bees to scare kids in the garden
No gardens, hardly anything can grow
Except indoors, protected from the toxic glow
The Vatican is covered in desert sand

2

You'll need your Earth Suit to walk outside
Cool skin under the thin metallic sheen
Keep that suit buttoned up
No one wants to be caught naked in the furnace
No suit, no air conditioning, and you only have minutes
Before you shrivel into sizzled bacon

The Earth Suit is a marvel of science
The material is almost invisible
Against your skin
Like the sheerest condom
The mask molds itself to your face
Some people never take it off
Some people say sex is much better
In the Earth Suit
Mass extinction will pass over our houses
We can smear our own blood on our doorways
We will be blessed
Humans will evolve into our Earth Suits
And we will be saved with new skins
Those who survive will be a lot smarter
Than me, and wiser too
Everyone else will die
Good luck

California Living

October 31, 2019

I don't know how to ski
But maybe I can ski down powdery smoke in Squaw Valley
I've been eating smoke for breakfast
And ashes for late-night snacks
We can watch *Up in Smoke* and maybe even laugh
Thinking of all the pot plantations perfuming our air
We can go to the dentist in the midst of huge flames
And sprawl in the burning chair
We can sing even when the opera house has become a torch
The Grateful Dead will be grateful no matter how high the
    flames
We have too many burning questions
For example, when they turn off the electricity
How do they milk all the cows without their milking machines?
Yanking the teats of hundreds of cows by hand?
What do we do when the breathing machine shuts down?
The newscasters are doling out information—
A list of schools that are shut, roads that are blocked—
But no one can see it, since the power is out
Except for those who do not need the information
The museums have been encased in fireproof performance art
The paintings have been sent to the stars for safekeeping
We all evacuate and then evacuate again
We can sing: *Open your Golden Gate*
And let the smoke escape
We can sing: *I left my lungs in San Francisco*
Thank you for your service Mr. Tony Bennett
California can now become the ash-heap of the future

Holiday Greetings 2019

December 14, 2019

A girl will lead us
A girl provokes the bullies of carbon
A girl gives Trump the willies
The world learns Asperger's is a superpower
Time magazine says she's the Person of the Year
Trump boils in jealous rage and mocks her
She mocks him back
Bolsonaro calls her a brat
And strikes a match to the Amazon
A girl will speak wisdom
To a room full of clowns
She's a fool, but not a laughingstock
She's a fool for God
Or whatever you think hovers over our heads
Or bubbles up from the Earth's core
But the girl is not the Messiah
She won't save us
Yet when we sing Handel's Hallelujah
During the holidays
We'll welcome her
To save us all
Happy 2020
If that's just one kid, imagine all the kids
Rising up and giving us a hand
A girl is not Hope but Hope is not lost
We are the ones who will bring gifts
To the Future stretched out in the hay of an old barn

PART TWO

CORONA CHRONICLES

2020

Our Social Distance

Shutdown begins

March 13, 2020

Stay away and be my love
We're so close together when we're so far apart
I take solitary walks with multitudes
I talk to myself but mostly I hear your voice
We follow each other at a distance
Songs ring down empty dark Italian streets
Windows of all the apartments fill with harmonies
Woody Guthrie is already singing the "Rambling Virus Blues"
Bach has written a new version of the Corona Variations
I can hear music winding through all the avenues
But there's no guitar and no piano in sight
We're all alone with each other
Keep your distance and make happy sex
Dance with each other in different continents
Everyone can be magnanimous and fart
And what our neighbors don't know won't hurt them
Let me be kind to you by way of Internet
Swimming through our brains
All alone we can open our doors
Yet keep away from each other
As far as any of us can spit
So keep your distance and be close
Speak splendid poems and deeper wit
Stay away and be my love

Shelter in Place

March 19, 2020

Shelter among the stars and gaze down
The contagion will come
And we'll be home
In the Milky Way
Some day
Right now our place is a weed
Squeezing through the cracks
We hang on despite the attack
Our shelter is being tender yet tough
Even if we have nothing but dirt
Hoping all that we can do is enough
We stare at our rugs, stoves, toilets, not much
But happy to notice our surroundings
To notice the weeds and how they thrive
That's our place, growing through the cracks
Find that place and stay alive

Flatten the Curve

March 22, 2020

How heroic are the grocery clerks
And the fast-food fry cooks
How brave are the ordinary workers
And the priests wandering through empty churches
How courageous are UPS drivers who risk their lives
How stoic are the cashiers and the bus drivers
And there's no way to thank them all
All will be well once we unbend the horizon
I weep when I see a happy baby
Blissful and unaware that the Angel of Death
Is trying to erase the ceiling of the Sistine Chapel
How tender are the smiles of life
How wonderful the professional calm of nurses
How sublime the persistence of doctors
How moving the faces of anxious waiting
How close we are in our distance
I want to use big words for such big feelings
But the words keep getting smaller and smaller
Flatten the curve and rise up

Out of an Abundance of Caution

March 25, 2020

Out of an abundance of caution
No one will die for a golf course
No one will sacrifice
For those made stupid by money
Out of an abundance of caution
No one needs to suffer fools
Science cultivates love and life
Tough knowledge gives hope
Out of an abundance of caution
Dreams wake up each dawn
And go back to work
Honest people know what to do
Even in the solitary dark
Out of an abundance of caution
The planet commands attention
And makes no excuses, tells no lies
Out of an abundance of caution
Walk as far apart from each other
And as close to the goodness
Of people as you can

We're All in This Together

March 29, 2020

Some of us are in this together
But there are also those who want to kill us
And we take secret shelter to flee
The pestilence and hate and greed
Living in Ann Frank's secret hideout
The real secret hideout
The one behind the closet
The one the Nazis never found
We don't hide from a virus only
The virus is a weapon wielded by those
Who decide we do not belong on their TV show
We hide from the entire mad network
Most of us are all in this together
The bottom has dropped out and we're falling
Into each other's arms, standing apart
Death herding us all together
Swabbing us all down with sanitizer
Not enough lifeboats
We're all in this together
And we have to decide who lives
We better speak to each other
We need to learn who we really are

The Great Toilet Paper Panic

April 1, 2020

Suddenly toilet paper becomes a star
Crowds chase rolls down the street
Like teenage girls chasing the Beatles in 1965
Panic sweeps through the land, a different type of virus
Without toilet paper our rectums won't be clean
And civilization will devolve into a stinky rash
We discover our bodies because of the plague
We may die alone, drowning in our own phlegm
But now we notice the obvious precious flesh
We all share bodies, we all inhale and swallow and shit
With Death silently circling around us
We reach deep into our sinews and bones
As if we discover them for the first time
And we exult in our commonality
Queen Elizabeth shits
Taylor Swift takes a shit
Jeff Bezos squeezes out his turds
The homeless man on the street corner takes a shit
You notice it because he shits out in public
But you know there's a world of sphincters
Hard at work behind closed doors
Hand them all a roll of toilet paper
Wiping ourselves clean is a moral imperative
And we share the great fear that there's none left
We will be abandoned, left to rot on our own
Making scatological jokes come true
So we grab all we can carry from the stores
We are afraid that our bodies will be taken away
We thought we were as solid as robots
But we are just soft bags of excrement
Trying to remember who we are
Trying to get a little comfort
Trying to hold a small sad piece of dignity
With a thin square of paper

Why Is This Night Different?

Passover

April 6, 2020

Why is this night different from all other nights?
Anyone got a good answer?
Maybe this night is different because
We are not in the Warsaw Ghetto launching our revolt
On the first night of Passover 1943
This night is different because
We are in our homes with family and friends far apart
Sharing a meal and songs on video screens
Breaking the matzo and toasting our wine
Planning on how we can launch our revolt
This night is different because
The Pharaoh is ignorant, venal, and cruel
And we are ordinary people who mourn
The dead in Queens and Gaza and Milan

This night is different because
There really is a plague
And it's coming after us
Skips the Pharaoh and his first-born
To force him to grant freedom to slaves
Instead, the plague lurks, looking for its prey
Seeking out a weak lung here and an old heart there
Hunting for nurses and bus drivers
Insinuating itself in the folds of our hands
So we must plan our revolt
With soap and water
To grab life for us all

This night is different because we can toss out
The fools and crooks and evildoers in charge
This night is different because
We have the power, together, to bring back our health
And reward us all with care for everyone
And once we are full, eating whatever rations we can find
Once we have tossed back our last glass of wine

We can then lean from each of our windows
Call out from our doors and across the balconies
Overlooking empty ghostly cities
We can shout with sadness and joy
That the quarantine and death are gone:

Next year dancing in the streets

Resurrection Day

Easter 2020

April 7, 2020

If Trump wants to really drive us crazy
He could shut down the Internet and we couldn't even
Wink and grimace at each other, cut off
With no outlet for our rage or love
No way to plot our revenge
But now news and songs are broadcast from homes
Everything has gotten very intimate
Newscasters and famous persons talk from
Bedrooms, home offices, dens, so far no toilets
Many of the commentators sit in front of bookcases
And I've taken to seeing if I can read the titles on the spines
Here's Plato's *Republic* and there's *The New Jim Crow*
Most of the time I can't make out the titles
Imposing hardbacks and well-thumbed paperbacks
On the wall a butterfly collection
That Nabokov would envy
A portrait of Muhammad Ali signed by the Champ
Alicia Keys sings a whimsical anthem
"Can't Come to My House"
Nobody can visit anyone
But she visits us one by one with her smile
So many solo acoustic performances
The cellist alone, the pianist alone
The stand-up comic without a fleshly audience
No laughs, no hecklers
It's Holy Week and maybe this time the pope
Will wash the feet of nurses and orderlies
Wash the feet of farmworkers living in shacks
Wash the feet of families of six living in two rooms
Impossible to find space to be separate
How do we forgive each other when we are so close?
So many dead in New York that mortuaries are too crowded
They say the dead will be buried in city parks
And we can't even enjoy the blossoms on the trees

Now we need to remember it's spring
Maybe we should try to remind the pope
Easter will come and we will rise again

Getting Affairs in Order

April 13, 2020

I'm trying to get my affairs in order
Millions are writing their wills
Saying goodbyes in advance
Once you land in the hospital it's too late
The virus strangles you, grabs your throat
And you can't pry those fingers off
No one's even there to comfort you
Except a stranger in a space suit
We have no choice but to be prepared for death
Fear fills the Safeway aisles
Tears flood the empty spaces of city streets
We need to get ready, use the dark dread as fuel
To get our final job done
So I'm trying to get my affairs in order
Even though the world is out of order

I admit that I can't get my papers straight
My last will and testament testifies to nothing
My health directive is a wish list of old films
Novels that I never read, songs I never heard
I give power of attorney to Lenny Bruce
Or maybe to Bruce Lee, either one will do
I give my children all that I can
Whatever cash, a house
And a future of sorrow and grace
Intense pleasure but also great pain
I give the sweetness of life
And my love for what needs to be done
The hard work of cleaning up

I bequeath all to my heirs
All the living things in my backyard
Dozens of roses about to bloom
Nubs of future plums hanging from the tree
Dangerous cactus needles scratching the sky
A baby redwood tree towering overhead

All the green flowering things that shelter with me

I'm so lucky to share in this small California space
I give them all
It's always when the bombs are about to drop
That you notice what the world can be
And what you want to leave behind

Ask Boccaccio

April 19, 2020

It's not the Black Death of 1348
People don't drop in their tracks
Farmers don't fall off their hoes
And die even before they hit the ground
Feral hogs don't root through corpses
Then keel over from the plague
(Ask Boccaccio—he knows)
It's not 1348, but it's terror nonetheless
At any moment the killer can strike
Maybe we can retreat to a hilltop
And tell stories, taking turns
Like Boccaccio's young refugees
Distracting ourselves from the horror
With stories of how foolish and wonderful people can be
Waiting for the plague to recede
Telling stories to keep us alive
New versions of the stories we thought we knew so well

We can tell the stories of strawberries and lettuce
Cucumbers and tomatoes and parsley
Of cheddar cheese and hamburger patties and chicken
    drumsticks
And who put them on our plates and how
The stories of those who work in danger and fear
Those who were invisible just last month
Tell the stories of those who are now suddenly essential
Those who are needed
Those who are unexpectedly important
Who pick and cut and bag and deliver
Tell the stories of the heroes of the disaster
And how much we love them
What if the essential workers get sick and die?
Who would pick the apples or lift the crates or drive the trucks?
Am I going to bend over to harvest artichokes?
Do I even know how to pull up carrots?
It's a fight for survival

And support for workers on the line is self-defense
Everyone else will live if the asparagus picker lives
That's the new story of our *Decameron*
Good pay, safe conditions, masks, gloves
Adequate housing, no crowded barracks
Protection from goons and harm and ICE
That's the song of the new social contract
The workers in the fields need to live
We're together because we have no choice
No one can be sacrificed because if they are
You are next
Ask Boccaccio—he knows
Don't ask Trump: he wants to cut their wages

Fear Itself

April 28, 2020

I'm afraid that my lungs will clog with super-cheap oil
I'm scared of secret virus flowers blooming on my feet
I'm scared of an elephant sitting on my chest
I'm frightened that The Great Leader wants me to drink Lysol
I'm afraid that he hulks over doctors and scientists
I'm scared that he tells us all is well when it's clearly not
I'm afraid he thinks war is a better cure than injecting Clorox
We can kill off millions quicker with a deft bombardier
We can stop the virus in its tracks with a surgical nuclear strike
On Tehran or Caracas or Albany or Sacramento
I'm afraid that the president has his eyes on the Dead Jones
    Index
He prays for the green light of the Dead Jones Index
I'm afraid of people marching with signs that say,
"Sacrifice The Weak"
I'm afraid that someone will decide that I'm The Weak
(I'm strong enough to take down at least one Nazi when they
    come)

I'm frightened that The Great Leader will bankrupt the states
I'm afraid that he will starve people, drive us insane
Make America Curse Again and Again
He'll deport the Cosmic Connection
Wipe off that solitary eye on the top of the pyramid
Render unto Caesar Pluribus Unum with interest
Declare a national catastrophe on top of a national emergency
Cancel the elections and declare that the country loves him
I'm terrified that he will still be around this time next year
I'd like to be afraid of fear itself
But that's not the case
I'm afraid of Trump

God Picks His Nose

April 30, 2020

God picks his nose and out comes a father or a mother
Ready to be rolled into a ball and tossed into the void
A teacher has perished, unable to deliver the lesson plan
The mail is now delivered to sepulchers
The mailman himself finally gets off his feet
Stretched out in his grave
Obituaries flutter like birds in the morning
Singing stories of mechanics and artists
Extraordinary lovers and ordinary neighborhood thugs

Every day more deaths, thousands adding up
The private hurt and the general horror
Individuals dead, real people with real teeth and lips
Each a palpable life filled with movies and food and standard-
    issue hopes
A middle-aged son of a friend, a brother of another, whole
    families
The ER doctor who kills herself because she can no longer bear
To witness deaths in the waiting room
In the front hallway, in the broom closet, everywhere
Like other battlefield soldiers
The doctor drops into the dark bottomless foxhole

Yet some deaths seem to have a cause, a location, even a mailing
    address
When the passenger coughs into the face of the bus driver
And two weeks later the bus driver dies
This seems to make too much sense
But others die plucked out of the herd, random selections
Abducted by microscopic UFOs with horns
There can be no herd immunity when there's no herd
Death with no contact and no apparent reason
People I know, others I would never know
An unbearable cascade that turns you numb

But then the tree begins to bear fruit
People of a small nation celebrate once again
That Vietnam defeated a giant invader

Several divorces are decided—correctly
Some loves are examined and renewed—correctly
A kid stuffs a giant sandwich in his mouth
The sun feels good after chilly clouds
Charlie Chaplin knows how to smile
A pregnant woman laughs with gusto
And we can scold God for picking his nose
"Keep your boogers to yourself,"
We tell him in solitary prayer
"It's not healthy any time but now more than ever—
God, clean up your act, and let us live"

Open Us Up

May 8, 2020

Trump wants America to open up
He wants *Open for Business* on every door
The beaches should be full, and the boulevards
Blasting with music
Love will be in the air, and so too Death
The President wants you to make a sacrifice
You're a Soldier in the battle to serve Great America Again
Dish out the pasta, stitch up the clothes
Get your nails done, and a haircut too
He wants to liberate America from Public Health
Public is not America
Very Private Health is America
We need to move on
We don't need to know how much, where, who
No tests, no tracing, no data, no models
If we act like everything is Normal
If we keep butchering Hogs
If Football is back in full frenzy
We can drive, eat, work, everything we want to do
All the Good Things of Life, sweet sex and intense chess
Such Beauty, as Imelda Marcos would say
Such Great Ratings, as Donald Trump still says
And now we await the results
Now that we are open wounds
Will waves of Death sweep over the land?
Will a Tesla worker collapse into a lithium bath?
Will the train conductor take tickets for Dry Cough, Wyoming?
Will the sausage maker from El Salvador
Get stuffed into America's breakfast?
Will Nebraska mourn at the Tomb of the Unknown Meat Cutter?
Will the Black clerk's fever defrost the frozen foods aisle?
We will all have the Honor to die
But some will be more honored than others
We are simply Tools
Waiting for our chance to serve
No time for sarcasm, much less for irony
Open us up like a heart transplant
Open us up like our first sexual awakening

Open us up like a stock market that knows better
Open us up like semi-automatics with beards

Refuge Enough

May 15, 2020

I look through the back door at my yard
Like peering through a tunnel or a portal to another world
Before me a patch of lawn
With bushes and roses and a redwood tree
And beyond my fence the railroad tracks
With few trains and fewer commuters
Traveling to yet fewer worlds
Between San Jose and San Francisco
And to the left the edge of a tiny studio
With memories and drafts of memories

This is my small refuge, and this is where
I think of the wife I've loved for 45 years
Touching and yearning from the first wet kiss
Through all the heartache and misunderstandings
Through surgeries and hard times and crazy kids
We knew the I-Hotel and Beirut
And other secret code words for tough struggles
We are so different, such contrasts in backgrounds
And after so many years we still don't know each other
The virus seeks to kill us both, circling around our green patch
Ready to pounce

Forced together as we await the monster
We have time to learn to touch again
To discover new continents in each other
To practice how to navigate oceans and archipelagos
To invent a new cartography of being close to harbors
To listen to old stories made new
To remember who we are and how we got here
To confess my love despite all the ways I have fallen short
How much I withdrew and forgot or became numb
I vow that I will be by your side no matter what we face next
No matter how much we and the world comes to grief
How the trains may carry us away to doom

I confess that I love you in ways that I do not yet know
And I may never know, but I will be by your side
Learning to be the one who deserves your love
And that is refuge enough

Check Back on May 22, 2021

May 22, 2020

Today is my birthday May 22, 2020
And my parents come to visit
Sitting on the couch after arriving from the dead
They whisper to each other
In Polish that I can almost understand
And they ask questions
"Are you careful to hide from the virus?"
And they tell me a story I know well
The story of the rabbi and his wife (my father's cousins)
How they hid in a farmer's attic
For four years to escape the Nazis
So they ask, "Do you think you can hide for four years?
For four months? Can you hide in the closet
For even four hours?"
And then they bring up my aunt's feats of survival
"Can you slide through the sewers to flee?
The way your aunt Zosia fled the Warsaw Ghetto?
Can you even wash your hands properly?
Do you know how to wear a mask?"
It's so wonderful to hear them, to feel their concern
How they nag me to steer clear of Death
Tell me that I need courage and luck
And how I must work for both
To hide from the virus
I thank my parents and assure them
That I will do all that I can
To get to my next birthday
To live to see Trump driven from the White House
To watch my grandchildren graduate and marry
All the typical joys of home and family
To survive the planet's growing rage
To forage for enough food to live
And to keep a simple sense of justice

Check back with me May 22, 2021
To see if luck and courage bring me here again

The Man Who Holds Up the Bible to Declare War

June 1, 2020

Did Trump just declare war?
The Strong Man clears the zone with his Federals
Tear gas and clubs and stun grenades
The Military Police clears his path
Peaceful protest swept away
He'll show those weak governors how it's done
The President walks through the debris
Takes his pose before the church
And lifts the Bible upside down into the air
God Wills It
Then he gathers his war cabinet for a snapshot
Knowing it or not they just co-signed the declaration
The moment has arrived as farcical theater
This was the first act of war
He calls for the US military to occupy the US
He declares that he is defending the Second Amendment
A signal to his militias that it's time to take out their weapons
We anticipated he would provoke martial law
As the election approached and he knew he would lose
Martial law is his re-election strategy
But who knew how it would come about?
In the midst of virus and vicious hatred
He puts his knee on millions of necks
He wants to shut us all up
He wants to round us all up
Remember all the courage and outrage
And the casualties we will now take
All the sick and dying filling the hospitals in a week or two
Now that the virus is running rampant
Among crowds who must take to the streets
But we can also see in those streets a hope
As young people of all types, all races, reach out for justice
And to rid ourselves
Of the man who holds up the Bible to declare war

401 Years to Find Ourselves

June 6, 2020

When Trump asks a general to occupy Minneapolis or Oakland
Will he say, "Sir, No Sir, I cannot violate the Constitution"?
Or will the general be made complicit in dictatorship?
Can Trump get the virus to stand at attention?
Can he get it to sweep the streets and attack only his enemies?
Can the tyrant get the virus to tear up
Those pieces of paper that promise freedom?
Troops with no insignias patrol Trump's world
But will the troops who come from our homes
Refuse to invade our homes?
401 years of slave patrols and shackles
But also 401 years of work and teaching and consciousness
401 years of Freedom Rides
And at last young people fill the streets
All races, all types, all hopes, all shouting
With practical rage and impractical joy
Learning the truth of America from those
Who know those 401 years too well
401 years and we've found us
401 years and we uproot the old plantation and the Indian fort
We transform the violence of settlers and masters
We take over our history and make an America
That belongs to the continent
With health and safety and pleasure and sustenance
Each of us equal and magnificent and just and free
And alive to inhabit all the streets with love

Third Reconstruction

June 6, 2020

First Reconstruction incomplete, got sold out
In favor of Jim Crow
Second Reconstruction rose up, gained ground
But was stymied and forced back
Now we got a Third Reconstruction
And we're getting the great rush of transformation
A rising up amidst great danger of virus and cops
And a tyrant chewing his nails wanting
To strike down all the building activity
Wanting to cancel all the 40 acres and digital mules
This time the country will be put on a sound foundation
One that starts to erase the color line
One that balances justice and wipes off the grin from killers
Young people are getting pragmatic
And desperate and effective, and it's such joy to watch
I'm so glad that I've lived long enough to see
The new generation taking over
Old folks can now pitch in
And be assured that someone knows what they're doing
Building on what came before
Planting flowers on our bones

The Compton Cowboys Hit the Trail of Found Dreams

June 12, 2020

The Compton Cowboys hit the trail of found dreams
Horses rule the meadows and groves of Oakland
Horses parade down Mission Street alongside Low Creations
Surfers gather in circles and ride waves of Aloha
To name George Floyd and all those murdered
Hawaii lifts up its heart to praise wonderful worlds again
Murals dance across all the faces of the world
And walls smile with fierce love
Even bold orange on the street to the White House
Black Lives Matter
Like lava flowing into people's souls
The wall surrounding the White House
Alive with posters and messages
Poems make sense of the universe
And the universe gives poems a reason to live
Such a wave, such a flow of magnificent power
All pulling the thread at the center of this country
Unraveling the centuries of horror
Slavery still raw, the daily humiliations, the strange fruit
A moment when people march and talk
Braving danger of the deadly virus, rushing forward
Riding our horses and making all the connections
Confederate flags no longer wave at NASCAR
Football's Commissioner sheds tears and promises to do better
Gone With the Wind went
Statues find themselves crashing to the ground
Generals apologize for being used by a vicious fool
A giddy reckoning drifts over the land
This is the moment, the Great Awakening
And there is more to come

A Juneteenth Traveler from an Antique Land

Juneteenth, 2020

The marble pillar that holds
A potted plant by my front porch
Is cracking apart, big crevasses tearing the rock
Falling to ruin and dust
So much for marble and immortality
No colossal wreck of Ozymandias, but I yet see
Vanity tumbling to the sands
And this crumbling marble announces
That the time has come
For America to split apart at the seams
In order to reconstruct itself as something even more solid
Uncle Ben is now "evolving"
According to his corporate family
And Aunt Jemima is on her way out
Juneteenth is a holiday most people never heard of
But now it's slicing the month
Between Memorial and Independence
Awareness contrasting when Emancipation was announced
With the long delay before the message is yet to be heard
Corporations are now rushing to correct images
They were too lazy to notice before
How many years before the country as a whole is free?
Equality demands more than retiring corporate mascots
Justice demands that nothing
Of the wrecked plantation manor will remain
No master's sneer of cold command
Only shattered ruins will stretch
Across lone and level sands

Born at a Time of Great Troubles

June 28, 2020

Welcome to the world, Grandson Ari
Born June 25, 2020 Chicago 6 lbs. 14 ounces
You've come at a time of great troubles
A terrible disease rushes across the country
A crazy strongman from Queens fights for the Confederacy
Cops still kill Black people almost at will
Millions out of work, out of food, out of time
And it all seems to be getting worse

It's a time of great troubles
But there are gifts for you
Millions in the streets making something new
Young people take risks to demand change
Black lives really do matter
The uprising will defeat the Confederacy once and for all
Statues fall and hopes rise
Public Health is the Party of Life
White supremacy is a public health issue
So is poverty, so are schools, so is a house, so is rape
So is a cop's knee on a Black man's neck
These young people are going to be your leaders
And you will be as creative in revolt as they

It's a time of great troubles
But also of great joy
Welcome to the world
We love you
We need your help

No Masks for the Party of Death

July 13, 2020

No masks for the Party of Death
They dance in crowded swimming pools
Their young faces are naked
The music pounds
They jump up and down in the water
Is this what the Bible calls *fleshpots*?
The beer flows, the party's never done
And the virus is glad to join the fun
It snakes among its victims
A parasite looking to chew some lungs
Or chomp a heart
And worse is yet to come
Ignorant and stupid and arrogant
Trump allows the sacrifice of multitudes
The Great Leader demands
That the kids go back to school
While he tosses paper towels into the ICUs
But the Strong Man is weak against a bug
He can't insult the invisible
He can commute the sentence of his buddy
Weird Stone
But the virus won't commute his own
We need to survive, hold on
As Protest and Providence
And Hubris bring him down

Virus Fires

August 28, 2020

Giant fires burn all around us
Smoke wafts through the trees
And the sky is a grim metallic color
Thousands of lightning strikes
Set "complex" fires, multiple hits
That spark and then combine
And radiate in all directions
Santa Cruz Boardwalk rollercoaster
Outlined at night by flames
Our lungs fill with ashes and disease
The president mugs like Mussolini
Sucks safety and freedom from our veins
Will he still be drilling into our brains for years to come?
The fires sweep across California
Huge hurricanes boil across the Gulf's hot water
Trump puts on his convention show
Touting Law and Order and All is Well
A Black man shot 7 times in the back in Kenosha
In front of his three sons
A white kid with a long gun kills two more
Hailed as a hero by too many
Flames of all kinds run wild in Reality TV Hell
Trump has found his Reichstag Fire
The country hangs in the balance
Basketball players in their bubble
Refuse to dribble
And they weep
"It's amazing to me why we keep loving this country
And this country does not love us back"
Millions produce chronicles
The outcomes of our grief
T-shirts with seven bullet holes in the back
Poems and diaries and photos and videos
Testifying that this is the moment
This is the time
We take note
We are aware
We watch the flames and furor

Embrace each other in love and horror
And do what needs to be done

Giant Orange Sky

September 9, 2020

Will anyone years from now understand
Or care about this moment September 9, 2020?
How do we survive a sky that's such
DEEP TOTAL ORANGE?
ORANGE STREETS ORANGE HILLS ORANGE FEET
ORANGE LIPS ORANGE BAY ORANGE BRIDGE?
Luminous ominous orange beauty
Can we put out all the fires?
Are we on the cusp of civil war?
Or has the civil war already begun?
How did we get lost in our own birth canal?
Where do we put our feet when there is no ground?
Who will breathe what we exhale?
What hopes have we squandered?
How many ventilators do we need if we never exhale?
Should I wait to write this poem until after the election?
Will I know who won by November?
When do these chronicles come to an end?
In November or January?
Or will they end in 2024?
Or when the fires are out?
When do we beat back the Boogaloo Boys?
How do we throw off **THE GIANT ORANGE SKY?**
ORANGE EYES ORANGE FEAR ORANGE DEATH?
Will this chronicle end after the plague has gone into hiding?
After I go into hiding?
We know the plague will never really go away
It goes into hiding like an angry rejected messiah
And it's ready to pounce back at any time
A persistent hidden malignancy like Nazis
I stare at the all-encompassing **ORANGE SKY** and hope
We can put out all the fires

RBG for a Blessing

Ruth Bader Ginsburg dies on Erev Rosh Hashanah

"May her memory be for a blessing"

September 18, 2020

RBG bless this day our daily hope
Let her memory be a shield
RBG protect us from harm
May her memory ignite
Young girls and boys to act
Let her story be an example
RBG live like her
May we make a planet worthy of her
May we remember all that she has done
And all that we should do
May her memory stop being undone
May her memory be a rocket ship for truth
May all the lies fall away
As she smiles at us from sky's memory
May her memory give relief
May her memory give strength
May she soar as a diva
And we listen to her lucid aria
May her memory allow us
To outlive the virus
To put up with a lot of shit
Put up with smoke and flames
Put up with bizarre fake conspiracies
May her memory let us sing and dance
With patience, cunning, and courage
May her death be for a blessing on Rosh Hashanah
And every year may Creation
Weigh our souls
May RBG measure all our deeds
With equal justice
And may RBG
Bless us with her memory

The Plague Chooses the Pharaoh

October 2, 2020

The plague chooses the Pharaoh
But the Exodus has yet to begin
Trump is in the hospital
The smoke level is too high
Day after day
And my lungs flutter
Bronchial butterflies
Inhaling dense smoke inside my bedroom
Fire circles around Calistoga
And the grapes and hot springs of memory
While the disease floats across the country
And the country floats across
All of Pharaoh's delusions and lies
And the smoke drifts through our lives
Yet we still remain enslaved
We could sing this in a prophetic voice
We could chant how the monarch has fallen
Because of his foolish reckless swagger
How hubris found its match in the virus
And how the very high have been brought low
By smoke and virus and Nazis
Such is the story of Trump
Like a biblical admonition
Vanity is not the road to life
And Creation wants the people to live
When he gets well
Send Trump to California
To sweep his forest floor

Running to Zamboanga

October 17, 2020

I am running in a panic through the Philippines with my wife, Estella. She was born there and knows her way around. We are fleeing some kind of an invasion. Have the Japanese returned? Are the Americans coming back? Has Spain sent the Armada? We keep running, afraid, and then we see a sign on the road: Zamboanga City. That's at the tip of the Zamboanga Peninsula on the island of Mindanao. Zamboanga City is the very end of the line, the last stop before the sea on one of the southernmost islands of the archipelago. We have nowhere to turn. That's when I feel the utter terror of being cornered.

It's just weeks before the election, and Trump gets more and more bizarre. Now he's a survivor, immune, he's found the cure, and he's able to jump into crowds and smother the ladies with kisses, he's a superhero, and he's coming after us in Zamboanga to smother us with thugs. The dread and low-grade persistent depression and the bizarre ideas are normal responses to catastrophe, even as I can see the world unraveling in front of me. But normal responses also include resilience and ingenuity and lots of laughs, Charlie Chaplin on the ledge about to fall but wobbles back.

Someone's pounding on the front door in the middle of the night. I jump up and grab the crowbar I keep by the side of the bed. They've broken in, and they're coming after us, more and more of them breaking through the door. But there is no one, and I put the crowbar down. Yet I keep feeling that someone has violated my home. All day I feel off-kilter, apprehensive, my planet tilting off its axis. I must be spooking myself. That morning the local TV news reports on burglars breaking into homes at night in our neighborhood even with the residents inside. I was right, even though I was wrong. I don't think I have ESP, just vast powers of anxiety. It's time to head for Zamboanga.

Zen Bookends

For Sojun Mel Weitsman Roshi
and Hozan Alan Senauke

October 25, 2020

In summer 1968
I walk with my friend Alan
To meditate at the Berkeley Zen Center
We sniff tear gas in the air
And see police roaming the streets
Abbot Mel hosts the meditation
Gentle and kind, a saving soul in deep silence
No sirens, no nightsticks
The world in turmoil
Yet also glimpses of another way
No need to explain, simply say, "1968"
Mel opens the space on the wall for Emptiness

52 years later
I return to the Berkeley Zen Center
To have lunch with Alan
Hozan Alan is now Vice-Abbot
And Abbot Mel is now 91
He is stepping down from his position
And Alan will step up later in the year
In a Mountain Seat Ceremony
I have not seen Mel for half a century
And we say hello and chat
The visit now and the visit then are bookends
To one shelf of an endless library

Weeks later I watch on the Internet
The stepping down ceremony for
Sojun Mel Weitsman Roshi
Retiring at long last
Stepping down as Abbot
He is tender and smiling
Joking sweetly
The world in turmoil
The virus digging into our flesh

And hatred and violence digging into our souls
But there's also hope only days before the election
No need to explain, simply say, "2020"
Mel opens the space on the wall for Silence

Blue Moon Halloween

October 31, 2020

Strange Halloween with kids in costumes
Of Public Health and President Death
Just days before the election
The Virus wiggles down the street
The Good Sane Doctor tries to speak
Great costumes with chirping kids
All tricks, no treats
"No virus no more," President Death declares
Without a hint of a reggae beat
Dumbfounded, Public Health just stares
Strange Halloween with a Blue Moon
Not just the song, although the song is great
But two full moons in one month
Not impossible but an oddity
Not really blue, although we hear the blues
Blue Moon
Without a love of my own
Next the clocks get all pushed back
According to the authorities of Time
Our heads are scrambled, our bodies off track
Then *Día de los Muertos* arrives
With all the memories of those who are gone
Dancing skeleton and grinning skull
Everything crashing forward to our Election
Will the sky fill with orange and red again
Or will *the moon turn to gold*?

PART THREE

TESTIMONY

November 2020–January 2021

On the Day Biden Was Declared President-Elect

November 7, 2020

We have a large empty birdcage on our back deck. Its previous tenant had died, and it's there for storage. The doors to the birdcage are shut. I can see the cage through the window of my office. Today a bird, perhaps a sparrow, was flapping around inside the cage. How the hell did he get in? Surprised, I went out and saw that the cage doors were closed, but there he was. I opened one of the doors and he shot out. How strange.

Surge

November 13, 2020

In a great cavernous hall I see all my dead friends. She died of breast cancer, that one was hit by a car while riding his bike, he succumbed to the virus, another was blown to bits but comes to me with his body intact, a dear mentor gone after years of Parkinson's, on and on. Ermena, Les, Diane, Nancy, Paul, Lora, Jay, Ted, Barry . . . You live long enough and you have a lot of dead friends, and behind them I can see the endless dead of the world.

Suddenly I feel an immense presence, a heavy weight on the whole space, a pressure bearing down on my face, my chest, in all my bones. It becomes clear, somehow, that I'm in the presence of God. But I see no form, no old graybeard, no young man brown Jesus, no blazing bush—there's just that great, heavy presence. I realize that this huge pressing weight is God. God is all of these many dead. Their total being makes for the Supreme Being. Not super-natural but all-too-natural. And over time the Deity is likely to grow even greater, and not too long from now I'll join the divine crowd.

Joy Then Dread

November 19, 2020

After great joy, a great sadness comes. After a dance around the house that Biden will take the job and everything will be OK, I'm overcome with more dread. I realize that Trump will not go away, and not enough will change. The election was just a juncture, not a conclusion—crucially important but not decisive.

The nurse in South Dakota says that their last dying words are "This can't be happening. It's not real." They insist that they're not dying from the virus but from the flu, lung cancer, anything but the virus. How can COVID be true? How can this not be a hoax?

Trump will tell his cult that he's been robbed, that Biden is not legitimate, he "won" because Black people voted for him, and Black votes are not real. And when he does step down, he's going to leave a wasteland behind, maybe hand over to the new president a raging war, gum up the works as much as possible, launch a coup of roadblocks and sinkholes, leave mountains of dead.

The nurse says, when it's time to die, "they're filled with anger and hatred. It just makes me really sad. I just can't believe that those are going to be their last thoughts and words."

Zoom Thanksgiving

November 30, 2020

Thanksgiving weirdly comes
Hurry up, the kids and grandkids will be here soon
No, they won't, no one's coming
The virus keeps us apart
But we can eat together on Zoom
Thank you, Food
Thank you, Internet
Thank you, Native People, for surviving murder and theft
Thank you, Black Lives Matter, for surviving murder and theft
Thank you, Quarantine, for keeping us alive
Thank you, Voters, for doing something right
Thank you, Dear Screen, for bringing us together
San Francisco, South San Francisco, Palo Alto,
Oakland, Los Angeles, Roseville, Milwaukee, Chicago
Seeing all the boxes
Makes me want to smell everyone
I want to see Isaac splayed on the couch snoozing
Ditto Donny in a food coma snoring
To watch Stella get out the ukuleles and Cherie do the hula
It's not the same, but Internet Turkey has its charms
Where else to watch Amethyst curl her hair in LA
Or Martha explain how it took a year
For her bones to heal in Oakland
Or Peter casually mention how lucky
We're all to be alive in San Francisco
Or watch Kayla bake cupcakes in Milwaukee
Or see the family tableau at the turkey shawarma feast in Chicago
With 5-year-old Eli grinning at everyone
Most of all, baby Ari watches Zoom boxes on his high chair
At 4 months old he's the youngest of us all
And now he can see his Grandma and Grandpa on a screen
Making silly faces and noises that grownups do for babies
One day we'll be able to hug him and smell him
Inhale that cheese neck and sniff his diaper
But for now we can only hug ourselves
And put up with our own stale aroma
Thank you, Future

Mysteries of Pandemia

December 2, 2020

My habits and desires have changed after months of isolation in Pandemia. I suddenly developed a taste for warm Diet Dr. Pepper soda. What a surprise. No ice, room temperature, a warm syrupy beverage some people might think is disgusting. I don't know why this drink suddenly became my favorite. I also stopped watching cable news all the time. I would turn the TV on in the middle of the night to see if 3,000 more votes were counted in Maricopa County or what wild demon would escape Trump's mouth. But suddenly I was no longer glued to the screen. I am able to turn off the TV and live in silence for long hours. Silence is definitely a change.

I have been learning how to read again, skipping the words. I've also gotten into a habit of speaking with objects around the house. I greet my favorite spoon and fork, the spoon so large and oval and the fork with a great bulbous handle. I thank the Japanese bidet for electronically saluting when I walk into the toilet; the lid lifts up to attention every time, and I salute back. I reason with the roses in the backyard. I greet the redwood tree every morning. (It's big and tall and hard to avoid.) I also have lengthy conversations with dead people— and I don't think I'm the only one who does this. I don't have any idea what day of the week it is. All days are the same. Which month? I forget to pay bills, and I'm not alone. I love my wife—we're stuck together, trapped on the same lifeboat—and this is the time to work out all our problems. Or kill each other. Other couples do the same. This is why I'm learning how to read, but without words.

I had a dream within a dream in which I woke up to discover that I was a Black woman getting ready to go to work at the grocery store. This is odd because I'm descended from Polish Jews. So in this dream I went back to sleep and had a dream that I woke up to realize that I was a white teenage boy in high school in Tulsa. Each time that I woke up in the dream I marveled to discover my new body. Breasts, hair, youthful muscles, genitals, unfamiliar hands. I've never been a woman, much less a Black woman; and I've never been to Tulsa. Back to sleep, and I wake up again but this time as a young Chinese woman jogging through the park. This goes on for a while, as I turn into dozens of different people, until I finally wake up from the dream of a dream of changing into yet another body. I get out of bed and look at the mirror, greatly disappointed: I'm a shriveled up chubby old white guy, after all. I'm not as interesting as the people I met—or inhabited—on my world flesh tour.

Stay Home

December 10, 2020

The tall green cactus in my garden stands upright, arms outstretched like a lanky green man, except it has long needles sticking out on all green sides instead of beards or pubic hairs, freckles or birthmarks. Some humans are prickly, but not like this. The cactus doesn't move, just stands with his sharp needles and waits for any intruder to get too close. Falling leaves from the tree beside it get pierced like butterflies on display, the leaves fluttering, helpless, as the cactus simply stands still and stabs them. The cactus is wise in the art of war: stay put and wait for the enemy, then jab him good without moving an inch. The cactus waits, the cactus wins, and I salute the cactus.

The virus sweeps across our county; there's so much that people who are infected no longer understand how or where they got it: the virus is everywhere. The doctors tell us to stay put, stay home. If the rush of people moving around stores and restaurants gets slow, then the virus won't be able to find you and swarm down your nose and throat. It's not so much place as traffic: stay home, far away from other humans, away from the swarm. This is where philosophical contemplation of the cactus becomes useful. Stay still, and let your needles stab the virus. Stay home.

Read Ron Padgett Poems Out Loud

December 12, 2020

"Waiting for Vaccine," by Samuel Beckett, is playing in my brain. Stay home and hurry up. "Exit Trump," by Rod Serling, is on TV. Soon the madman will be gone, unsure of what's real. He's trying his slow-motion coup attempt, punching out one lawsuit after another, losing them all, even his stacked Supreme Court couldn't help, failing in all respects. Now he's moving on to get officials in key states to void the vote. It's not a legal strategy; he's trying to engineer his conspiracy theories, and these court cases are to be used as building blocks in a paranoid story line for his raving followers. Trump's cult waits for his orders with the danger of violence mounting. There's no need to fill the streets with people trying to stop him, at least not yet. But I'm ready; it's not over. Cue the weird *Twilight Zone* music. Stay home.

So, we're home, waiting. We're stocked up on food, and we've got some money, thanks to Social Security and pensions. We're not starving like so many who are lining up to pick up bags of food at the pantries. We're lucky. And we have many ways to be busy. For example, I've begun reading poems out loud to Stella as she's tucked in bed trying to sleep. It's a little like reading a bedtime story, except the stories are by Keats or Blake. On to Edna St. Vincent Millay and Langston Hughes. After about one or two poems Stella falls asleep - the lull of meter and rhyme does the trick very well - although I keep reading out loud for my own pleasure. But when I read poems by Ron Padgett, Stella laughs, snorts in delight. You can't fall asleep when you laugh. So, after a couple of poems I'll switch to a Shakespeare sonnet and she'll doze off. Stay home, and read Ron Padgett poems out loud.

Missing

Winter Solstice

December 21, 2020

An older woman in the parking lot of the supermarket was crying, her tears rolling down to her mask. People gathered around her, at a distance, and someone asked her if she was OK and why was she crying. She pointed to the Christmas decorations, lights flashing, a decorated tree, Rudolph's red nose, and all the rest. "I miss Christmas. All of this"—she pointed at the holiday lights—"don't make up for hugging my grandkids. I'm alone. The phone's not enough." And all of the people sighed. The sigh contained millions of regrets and losses tumbling out of their souls. They had come to console her, but they needed consolation themselves.

For a second everyone in the parking lot was swept up in shared sorrow, everyone stopped, remembering all that they were missing. And the silent roll call of loss went like this:

Missing my senior-year trip to Spain. Missing my belly-dance class. Missing my job, missing my paycheck. Missing grandma, and grandma's missing me. Missing Zumba, missing Spanish class, missing teachers in the flesh. Missing God coming to visit me in huge crowds in Macy's. Missing my chorus, no Handel this year. Missing a big feast, missing food, missing sitting in a fancy restaurant or a greasy spoon. Missing going to a basketball game, missing the way people crowd into a movie house, sniffing each other before the film starts. Missing the tongue of flame that would sweep up a prophet. Missing my love, now gone, missing my brother, dead, and my friend, succumbed, missing grandpa dying alone. Missing latkes and chicken soup with friends at my house, missing the tamales my aunties would make. Missing sitting in a coffee shop and reading a book or scrolling down my laptop, watching everyone milling around. Missing the stand-up comedy club, and all the insult comics lambasting Christmas, missing *The Nutcracker*, missing the kitsch. Missing the way people are smashed together watching the fireworks on New Year's Eve. Missing the touch of my kids far away.

And then the brief interlude ended, and everyone dabbed their eyes, adjusted their masks, and someone in the crowd told the grandma who was weeping that she wasn't alone. All of us are missing a lot, and we never know how precious it could be to do all the normal things until they are taken away, but everything was going to be much better next year, we'll be free of the virus then, a madman will not be in the White House, we just have to hold out, stay steady, wait for the vaccine. That was a happy lie to make us forget our sorrows, and even though we all knew it, we were comforted, and we wished with all our hearts that it would all come true.

Stand for the New Year

December 31, 2020

People are so glad that miserable 2020 will be behind us. But what makes us so sure it will be gone? Only on January 20, when Biden is sworn in, will 2021 begin. That will really be a new year. Or maybe when the pandemic is throttled once and for all, maybe in 2022? 2023? Perhaps we're lost in a maze of our own making. Grief and fear stretch across the country. Time gets stretched out too, cooped up at home, and maybe 2020 never ends. The decade will be known as the Roaring 20 (no 20s, just one long 20).

Maybe the Y2K glitch has arrived 20 years too late. I look at the digital calendar on my smartphone and the date reads, "December 32, 2020." We may be trapped in a glitch of time.

But then I talk with the redwood tree in my backyard.

Scientists have learned that trees in forests communicate with each other through fungus attached to their roots. They talk to each other. The Tree of Life is actually a Forest of Life. A lot of "primitive" people have known this for a very long time. Trees don't need to move around, they are separate above the ground. But underground is another story. Fungus connects one root system to another and then to another and another. The trees share nutrients and information between each other.

The redwood tree in my backyard is probably hooked up to the nearby maple and grapefruit trees, and even to the squat palm below the loquat tree, and of course to the plum tree. I asked the redwood what next year would be like. The redwood consulted with all the other trees. I waited but I didn't hear or feel anything that would be an answer and turned around, walking to the back door of my house.

What do I expect from a tree? My athlete's foot rash is not the same fungus that connects all the trees, so there's no way to communicate. Besides, what does a redwood tree know about years? The revolving and spinning of the Earth the tree understands, the change of seasons, the sun, the mist, the buds and plums, the fires, that's what time is to a tree, not the flipping of calendars humans make.

But then I sensed it just as I reached the back door. I felt a flash of revelation and turned around. I looked up at the tall tree, and I understood. The tree just stands. One redwood near our house is over a thousand human years old; my redwood tree is not that old but old enough to be wise.

Keep standing. Don't fall.

Witness

January 25, 2021

After he was sworn in, we went out on our porch and shouted and whooped. Stella beat a Pueblo hand drum and we waved, hollering that Joe Biden is President! Nobody on the street; no one walking by. Maybe they were all watching the inauguration on TV. One of our neighbors had put up an American flag. Silence. But I know there is great joy in streets around the country. I'm still suffering trauma from the sacking of the Capitol and four years of Trump's "American carnage." Enough. Ordinary days to come, and still so many problems, so much disease, including the fever of an empire in decline.

During this hard time, we witnessed all sorts of new phrases and behaviors: social distancing, sheltering in place, dying alone. What was once unfamiliar and strange ("flatten the curve") has become common, even banal, demanding a poem. Language has to keep up.

We witnessed four years of Trump's reign, four years of troubles, shootings, wildfires, racial reckoning, planetary murder, plague, monumental lies, alternative facts, #MeToo, an uprising for justice, and more. But a failed far-right insurrection had to be the capstone of these terrible times, and the nation is not done yet. War has broken out between those who follow the Text and those who follow the Man, between the Constitution and the Cult.

There is hope, though, a new administration, but the way won't be easy. The virus mutates and the war over reality continues. Now follows a time of uncertainty and struggle, fear and sickness mixed with love and joy, requiring another chronicle beyond these past four years.

One final dream: I'm in a room and I suddenly realize that I own copyrights on all gaps of knowledge. Any time there's a hole in what's known, in any field or practice or cosmology, I collect royalties. The gaps are innumerable. Ignorance is making me rich. I'm stunned. In my dream I see Mark Twain, and he's proud.

About the Author

Hilton Obenzinger writes poetry, fiction, cultural criticism, and history, for which he has received the American Book Award and other honors. Born in Brooklyn, he graduated Columbia University in 1969, taught on the Yurok Indian Reservation, was part of a collective community printing press in San Francisco's Mission District, worked as a commercial writer of training programs, co-edited a periodical on Middle East peace, and taught writing, literature, and American studies at Stanford University. In 2020 he retired as associate director of Stanford's Chinese Railroad Workers in North America Project. He lives in Palo Alto, California, and is married to the historian Estella Habal.